ULTIMATE COMICS
SPIDER-MAN

WRITER: **BRIAN MICHAEL BENDIS**

ARTIST: **DAVID MARQUEZ**

COLOR ARTIST: **JUSTIN PONSOR** WITH **PAUL MOUNTS** (#28)

LETTERER: **VC'S CORY PETIT**

COVER ART: **DAVID MARQUEZ** WITH **JUSTIN PONSOR** (#23 & #26-27) & **RAINIER BEREDO** (#24-25 & #28)

ASSISTANT EDITORS: **EMILY SHAW** & **JON MOISAN**

EDITOR: **MARK PANICCIA**

COLLECTION EDITOR: **JENNIFER GRÜNWALD**

ASSISTANT EDITOR: **SARAH BRUNSTAD**

ASSOCIATE MANAGING EDITOR: **ALEX STARBUCK**

EDITOR, SPECIAL PROJECTS: **MARK D. BEAZLEY**

SENIOR EDITOR, SPECIAL PROJECTS: **JEFF YOUNGQUIST**

SVP PRINT, SALES & MARKETING: **DAVID GABRIEL**

EDITOR IN CHIEF: **AXEL ALONSO**

CHIEF CREATIVE OFFICER: **JOE QUESADA**

PUBLISHER: **DAN BUCKLEY**

EXECUTIVE PRODUCER: **ALAN FINE**

ULTIMATE COMICS SPIDER-MAN BY BRIAN MICHAEL BENDIS VOL. 5. Contains material originally published in magazine form as ULTIMATE COMICS SPIDER-MAN #23-28. First printing 2014. ISBN# 978-0-7851-6706-8. Published by MARVEL WORLDWIDE, INC., a subsidiary of MARVEL ENTERTAINMENT, LLC. OFFICE OF PUBLICATION: 135 West 50th Street, New York, NY 10020. Copyright © 2013 and 2014 Marvel Characters, Inc. All rights reserved. All characters featured in this issue and the distinctive names and likenesses thereof, and all related indicia are trademarks of Marvel Characters, Inc. No similarity between any of the names, characters, persons, and/or institutions in this magazine with those of any living or dead person or institution is intended, and any such similarity which may exist is purely coincidental. **Printed in the U.S.A.** ALAN FINE, EVP - Office of the President, Marvel Worldwide, Inc. and EVP & CMO Marvel Characters B.V.; DAN BUCKLEY, Publisher & President - Print, Animation & Digital Divisions; JOE QUESADA, Chief Creative Officer; TOM BREVOORT, SVP of Publishing; DAVID BOGART, SVP of Operations & Procurement, Publishing; C.B. CEBULSKI, SVP of Creator & Content Development; DAVID GABRIEL, SVP Print, Sales & Marketing; JIM O'KEEFE, VP of Operations & Logistics; DAN CARR, Executive Director of Publishing Technology; SUSAN CRESPI, Editorial Operations Manager; ALEX MORALES, Publishing Operations Manager; STAN LEE, Chairman Emeritus. For information regarding advertising in Marvel Comics or on Marvel.com, please contact Niza Disla, Director of Marvel Partnerships, at ndisla@marvel.com. For Marvel subscription inquiries, please call 800-217-9158. **Manufactured between 7/25/2014 and 9/1/2014 by R.R. DONNELLEY, INC., SALEM, VA, USA.**

10 9 8 7 6 5 4 3 2 1

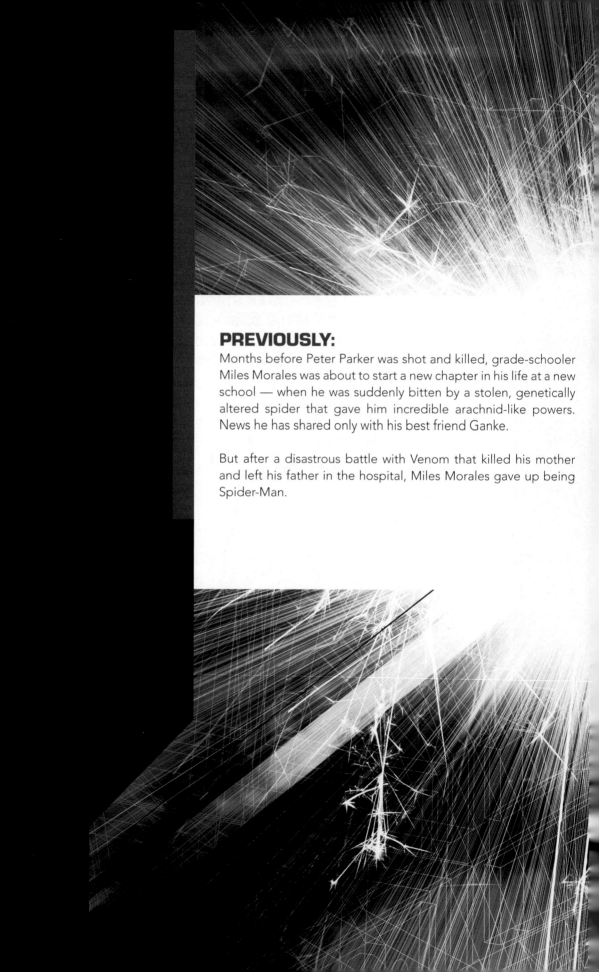

PREVIOUSLY:

Months before Peter Parker was shot and killed, grade-schooler Miles Morales was about to start a new chapter in his life at a new school — when he was suddenly bitten by a stolen, genetically altered spider that gave him incredible arachnid-like powers. News he has shared only with his best friend Ganke.

But after a disastrous battle with Venom that killed his mother and left his father in the hospital, Miles Morales gave up being Spider-Man.

You know, Legos.

Legos, the little--Legos the toy?

Yes. The little bricks?

It's a limited edition.

Legos.

It was the Triskelion with President Captain America being sworn in limited edition--

Edition. Yeah.

YES!!

I'm sorry.

Thank you!

So, uh, I'm going to go to my room and, let's say, e-mail my parents.

Yeah, okay.

See you after dinner.

Sure.

I ask for so little.

I think I'm going to tell her.

Tell her you love her?

What? No.

You haven't told Katie Bishop you love her yet?

No.

Girls like when you tell them.

Oh yeah?

She would.

You know what girls like to hear all of a sudden?

Sure.

This from the man who just chased another girl from our table crying over Legos.

That's not why she left. She had to e-mail--

Dude.

She had to go--

I promise you I don't know what girls want from us but I know they don't want to hear about you and the Legos.

The right girl will.

Wait, what were you going to tell her?

About, you know, who I was.

Whoa! Wait! Why would you do that?

Because I feel like it's part of my past and it's big and I don't like keeping it from her.

Huge mistake.

No, it's--

Huge.

Everyone told you, you *don't* tell your girlfriend you're a super hero.

Peter Parker *himself* told you.

All you do, at the end of the day, all you do is put them in *danger*.

But I'm not... *that person* anymore so--

You *are.*

You're just on a break.

I hate when you say that.

I hate when *you* say *that.*

And I'm right.

I'm really-- I need you to *respect* it.

I *do.*

I haven't said a peep in forever. *You* brought it up.

And I'm telling you I'm done.

I'm saying *that* is impossible.

Yo man, you're bummin' me out.

We'll see.

We *will* see.

We'll see *nothing.*

Jdrew:

Are you NOT coming?

Uh-oh.

Who is it?

It's, ugh!! It's Jessica Drew.

Who is *that*?

Spider-Woman.

I was supposed to meet her.

She just texted you?? Right now while we were just talking about--??

Now?

Yeah.

Why?

She probably wants to have the same damn conversation *we* just did.

And you blew her off?

I didn't mean to. I forgot.

Uh-huh.

You blew her off because subconsciously *you know* she will convince you *it's time.*

Dude, don't!

See you in the room.

Oh hey! See if she can get me the limited edi--

Not going to happen.

MILES:

I'm so sorry.

Jdrew:

Don't make me come down there.

MILES:

Where r u now?

Dad?

There he is.

How's work?

It was work? You home for dinner?

Sure.

Does the school know where you are?

Yeah, sure.

Go wash up. We'll order in Chinese.

We can go out. Give me a few minutes.

Let's, uh, let's go out.

A year is a long time. How many people could you have saved?

You fall off a horse, you get back on.

You ready?

Almost.

A doctor!! *I need a doctor!!*

Look at you.

Look what you can do.

I could go for some Chinese.

Let's find a place we've never been before.

So I heard from the lawyer.

You wanna cab it?

No. I'm supposed to walk whenever I can.

What did the lawyer say?

The police department isn't going to just settle.

Did we think they would?

Our lawyer thinks they eventually will.

They're going to write a check.

Like, for how much?

When this is done, college is paid for.

You're gonna tell me your mom wouldn't want that money going to your college education?

No way. I don't know if--

I just--

And we can take a trip. In style.

I mean, hell, we could just move.

Out of this city. We could move to England!

Move where?

Move to England?

Or Hawaii.

I get a call from school, they catch you guys mackin' on each other every five minutes.

That girl.

And, you know, other stuff.

You know what mackin' is.

Mackin'?

And a trip? How much are we getting?

A cop accidentally *shot* your mom while she was trying to help save sick people?

They're paying.

No one wants to see you or me on the stand.

Gimpy and sad eyes.

Which one am I?

We *should* take a trip.

Get out of this crazy city. Go see something.

Let's try there.

LUCKY CHANG'S

Welcome, welcome. Sit, sit.

I don't want to move.

I--I got stuff going on here.

She's-- it's not like that. She's cool. She's insanely cool.

Good to hear.

For a while there I thought you and the Gankster had a thing going.

What?

Frankly, your mother thought that years before--

Mom thought that Ganke and I were... *together*?

Nothing wrong with--

Ew.

Can I take your order?

Oh, uh...
um...
hey.

Hi.

You know each other?

Yeah, uh, where do we know each other from?

School.

Oh, yeah.

Yeah, you're the kid that-- uh, can I take your order?

I'm Jefferson.

Gwen.

What's good?

Uh, the duck.

Okay, duck for me.

He wants pot stickers and shrimp fried rice.

Something to drink?

Water.

You got Rolson?

I'll see.

What's the deal there?

No deal.

You'll excuse me.

Kid's got play all of a sudden.

Hey...

Gwen Stacy? You work here?

Sorry, sorry.

Yeah, um...

It's just good to see you. You stopped texting.

I just.

No, I get it. I do.

You're getting tall.

Am I?

Taller.

You okay? Your dad looks good.

Don't--don't say anything about anything.

Hey, come on, please. Like I didn't know not to say anything about anything.

Hey, listen, just--

I went through this too.

I lost my *dad.*

Spider-Man-related and everything.

I'm okay.

No, Miles, anyone can see that you're not.

And you, honestly you never will be. Not really.

This is going to be part of you forever.

I just wanted to say, don't hold it all in.

You can call me to talk about it or anything.

Okay? We're part of, like, this club.

Yeah, okay...

Everything okay?

Yeah. She's just--

You want to go?

Kinda, yeah.

Okay.

Okay?

Sure.

You "sure" sure?

We'll go.

Hey, miss, we have to go, actually.

You know what? I didn't see the time.

We'll have to cancel the order.

Really?

We cook for you.

We have to go.

What did you do?

She didn't do anything. It's the time.

Ah!

Miles?

Westwood Mall, Queens.

I'm the assistant manager. Can I help you?

Yeah, I'm actually *dying* of old age waiting for some fries and a water.

Oh, okay, here we go. Sorry for the-- hey...

I know you.

Yeah... I know you, too.

Where do I--?

You were at the national student council Hamptons' weekend.

Food Court
BURR-GERS GEN. CHO'S Chick-Chick-Chick'n

Oh my God!!

How long does it take to get french fries and a bottle of water?!

I'm sorry.

Th-they had to reboot the fryer so--

UGHH!!

I was.

You're student council president of Midtown High. The Spider-Man high school.

I am.

And we, uh, we don't really call it that.

Tandy. Tandy, right?

I'm student council president of Forest Hills High School.

Ty Johnson.

ASSISTANT MANAGER

Hi. Tandy Bowen.

Oh my God, Ty!!

This is *insane!*

Not bad, huh?

Can I tell you something?

You're not going to mention I got a limo?

Shut up and listen.

I-I never thought--

In my *life* I never thought I'd ever go to prom.

In fact, I resigned myself to the idea: there are people who get to go to--

You didn't think I was gonna ask you to your prom?

No. I'm saying *before* we met--

Before we met I never thought I would ever meet anybody that I--I felt this way about.

And I never thought I--I would feel--I just want you to know that this...

What you did here tonight...

You don't think I *knew* this?

I knew this was important to you.

Of *course* I was going to go all out.

And I'm saying--oh crap--if I cry I'll mess up my makeup.

Tonight is important to me too.

You don't like stuff like this.

Hey.

I like making you happy and I've never had a chance to make you *this* happy.

I would totally marry you right now.

Wow. Then I'm really glad I splurged--

For the--

DAILY BUGLE

PROM NIGHTMARE

Two New York City school class presidents lie in a coma after near fatal hit and run disaster.

page 4

High school seniors, Tandy Bowen and Tyrone Johnson were struck in a rented limo by a speeding delivery truck. The driver, Simon Marshall, was killed instantly. Both happen to be high school class presidents from competing neighborhood schools. The two were on their way to prom where they were both expected to...

New Spider-Man a Hoax?

See Editorial

Tony Stark Party Life Out of Con

Holy!!

Ho!!

Aaggh what the hell??

Miles! Are you okay?

My restaurant!!

Whoa!

Not my fault. Sorry.

Have you ever met these--?

Don't.

I'm whispering.

Shut up, Gwen Stacy!!

I've gone this long without my anti-super-hero father finding out I was Spider-Man.

I don't need you mouthing off in front of him.

We have to get out of here!

I'm not going to let him find out NOW especially when I'm not even Spider-Man anymore!!

I'll distract your father and you go--

Shut up.

Look at you!!

You rarely find things that are both.

They're half dead, Layla, what are you talking about?

Hell, Dr. Zola, everyone thinks *we're* dead, and I, for one, found it all very freeing.

It has made our work as the Roxxon Brain Trust all the more--

Freeing.

Yes.

You said it was time to get back to human testing...

God saw fit to provide.

Yipes!

Light lady and shadow dude...

Okay, whatever this is... I'm out.

I donaaaaa--

--aaaaaaah!!!

We should go.

The police.

What are you doing?!

She's going to explode out of you.

No. I have it now.

Oh, do you?

We are not violent people and we are smarter than this.

Well, I didn't know she could explode.

We knew she could do something.

She's not going to talk to us. Let her go.

She will. She has to.

I'm still not used to any of this.

I really don't think we ever will be.

Why-why did this happen to us?

I'm working on it.

Initiate phase 1 protocols.

Everyone at your stations.

Please make sure that all sensors and recording devices are *on* and calibrated.

Right now? This is happening right now?

That's what we called you in for, boss.

You have moved heaven and earth for us... it's the least we can do.

Really? *Right* now?

Process A engaged.

What are you injecting into the--?

Is--is-- is *that* dark matter?

It is a catalyst compound.

Vital signs are stable, Zola.

I think we are a go for Process B.

We already *have* dark matter inside of us.

Everything does. All things do.

It's the thing in between the things that make us *us*.

So is the *theory*...

You see...and I mean no offense, Mr. Roxxon, but the problem with your experiments up until now is that you keep trying to duplicate what Norman *Osborn* did.

What Norman Osborn created with his fractured Oz formula...

What the Parkers created with the symbiotes years ago...

Why would you try to duplicate failure?

Spider-Man was Osborn's penicillin, his accident...

But what it did show us, inarguably, was that there are energies inside all of us.

Untapped potential.

Things we can't even perceive yet.

Um, I think we have a--

Uh-oh.

No more.

Please...

SPIDER-MAN: NO MORE

Gwen??

Revoort
Realty
FOR SALE
Alison Blaire realtor

Gwen Stacy, why are you home so early?

Shouldn't you be at work?

Did you get fired?

No more work.

No. It's just that my work isn't there anymore.

The restaurant closed?

More like: random super-powered crazy people smashed it up, so it's not so much a restaurant anymore as it is a big pile of glass and rubble.

Goodness. Are you okay?

I'm losing faith in humanity, but other than that...

What happened?

You remember Miles Morales?

Do I remember the little boy with spider powers?

Of *course* I remember the little boy with spider powers.

Did you see him?

He came into the restaurant with his father.

And *he* destroyed the restaurant?

No.

No, he didn't do a thing.

He didn't help anybody. He didn't even try.

Gwen, he's just a boy--

We?

We-- we needed him, and he--

You and I!

We needed him to--?

To be *Spider-Man.*

Yes!!

Someone needs to be Spider-Man, and it's *him.*

He was our second chance.

We--we--we opened our hearts to him...

What did you *say* to him?

I slapped him in the face and called him a coward.

Oh, Gwen...

Right in the face.

And was it the best way to get good work out of good people?

It seemed so at the time.

Not everybody's cut out for such a dramatic life.

Maybe we should just let the boy grow up and decide what *he* wants to be.

Yeah, sure...

Oh my God!

Are you and Ganke not talking?

Don't worry about it.

Don't *worry* about it?

That's like a sign that the world's coming to an end.

How are you living in the same dorm room and not talking to each other?

I'm talking to him...he's just not talking to me.

What did you do?

Nothing.

Miles...

It's-- it's *his* thing.

It's a dude thing. Let him work it out.

Is it me?

Is what you?

Is he mad about you and me?

No.

Why would he be mad about--

Because, you know...

Know what?

You know he has kind of a thing for you, right?

What??

Well, he sure hopped off like a jilted--

No.

We'll see.

I-- listen--I know wh he's mad...

Because you're being selfish and--and a coward, and I've *had it!!*

Hey!

Miles, I mean it!

What?

I found out what happened at the Chinese restaurant.

You had a perfect opportunity to get in there and *do the right thing*...and you *ran away??*

Who told you that??

Gwen Stacy *texted* me.

Yeah...

You ran away.

To *help* my father!

The way she tells it, your father was already safe.

You *really* don't understand what's going *on* here?

You really don't get that I *lost my mother!!*

Okay??!!

SHE'S DEAD!!

And what was the last thing she said to you?

Was it: Don't be Spider-Man anymore?

No.

You told me she was **proud** of you.

Lots of people die, Miles.

And **you** are Spider-Man.

You need to help the ones that aren't dead.

You needed some time to shake it off, sure, but that time has **waaaaay** passed.

It's been **a year!!**

Think of all the good you could have done!

She died **because** of Spider-Man. My father will **never** be the--

You didn't kill her.

It wasn't even that big, giant, scary monster Spider-Man villain you were fighting...

It was a bullet.

A stray **police bullet** killed her.

I'm saying when you remember that day... maybe focus on all of the people whose lives **you saved** that night.

Including the life of your father.

You don't understand how this feels.

It must feel like an insanely big burden.

Yes! Like a giant responsibility.

It is.

That comes with the great power...

I know what you're doing.

I know you know what **I'm** doing.

What are **you** doing?

Everyone's **pushing me!!**

Because everyone **believes** in you.

Pushing me and **pushing** me!!

Miles!

YOU DON'T UNDERSTAND!!

I understand everything.

Except I don't get how-- how--don't you even **care** where these new super-powered kids **came** from?

YSTERY POWER TEENAGERS RANSACK BOROUGH

REFRESH FOR DETAILS

You did this to us?

Who *are* you?

Literally millions and millions of dollars have been spent to make this happen.

You were dead, and **we** brought you back to life.

You were nothing, and now *look* at you.

But *show* me!! *Show me* what you are!!

What the--??

Who are you??!!

What did you *do* to us??!!

Why??

Aaggh!! Black matter conversion.

I am loving what I am seeing-- *arghh!!*

Where is my mother??!!

Some sort of ÷coff÷ psionic light energy projectile.

Nnn...

Don't you hear me?! *Psionic light* energy!

But, the question is, are you *creating* it yourself, or *pulling* it from another source?

Powerful, powerful stuff.

Together, you have control over darkness and light.

AGAIN!

DAILY BUGLE

R HEATWAVE
t move north?

PAGE 3

MYSTERY POWER TEENAGERS RANSACK BOROUGH

see page 2

FORTUNE COOKIES
Not actually from Asia
PAGE 5

Brooklyn, Today.

Cloak and Dagger?

This ain't a library, kid!

Dad?

What you doing out here?

I was--I was headed home.

I just thought--

To see me?

You wanna try dinner again?

Sure.

Maybe we could have a meal without those awful lunatics ripping our world apart.

Maybe we order in?

Yeah, maybe... pizza?

Pizza always works.

Give me like a half an hour!

I just need to rest my eyes.

Yeah, no problem.

Jesus!!

You--you can't just *sneak in* here.

Of course I can. I just did.

How did you know I was going to be here?

I didn't even know I was coming here until--

You know who I work for, right? You know what I can do.

But!

You might want to keep it to a whisper--

Your dad's been through enough for one week, don't you think?

Last year you asked me what the connection was between you and me...

You asked me, and I told you that I wasn't ready to tell you.

That wasn't fair.

I'll tell you now if you want.

Okay...

A couple of years ago, some scientists with absolutely no moral center took DNA samples from Peter Parker and attempted to clone him.

And then they poked around at the DNA, just, you know, to see what they'd get...

Sorry for the intrusion, Miles.

Spider-Woman?!

God-- Why are you--?

Close the door.

You can't be here.

This is *insanely* uncool.

What?

You didn't throw it out.

I came to see if you threw out the new costume I brought you.

You didn't toss it or burn it or sell it...I'm going to take that as a good sign.

You can take it back.

I am one of the things they got.

You--

You're the *clone* of Peter Parker?

26

SPIDER-MAN- NO MORE

Queens. Today.

It's me.

It's *me!!*

It's Lori.

Yeah? You saw the news?

You're freaking out?? *I'm* freaking out.

They--they came out of *nowhere!*

No!! I don't *know* them!!

They called themselves Cloak *and* Dagger. *No!*

No. Come on...

I'm *scared* to go home.

I don't *know* if they're waiting for me inside.

Dude, I haven't been *in* a super-person fight since my mother went to jail when I was 15.

NO!!

I told you I don't *want* to be Bombshell.

My mother *made* me be Bombshell.

Please let me come over.

Be-because I don't have anywhere else to go...

And you're-- you're supposed to be my boyfriend.

But--

But I *need* you now.

So *that's* how it is?

Well, you can go straight to--

Sorry about that.

How much longer are you going to need, Dr. Sterns?

We are about there, Mr. Roxxon.

You can take a seat in the observation deck and congratulate yourself for being years ahead of Norman Osborn and his petting zoo.

Are you comfortable, Ms Baumgartner?

Do you know who Captain America was?

Was he a wrestler?

You kids today with your rock and roll...

No. He was a war hero. *The* war hero.

Oh yeah, okay, sure.

"Okay, sure."

Well, if all goes according to plan...

Today.

Maybe we're going about this all wrong.

Her name was on the Roxxon list.

Roxxon took everything from us.

They turned us into this.

We should go to your mother. Tell her you're okay.

No.

Maybe our families--

Ty... no.

Our families *sold* us.

Maybe they didn't know what they were--

Ty, it's just *us* now.

It's just you and me.

The police might--

You *know* it's just us.

You know that.

I know.

They took *everything* from us.

What happened to us will never happen to anyone *ever again*.

We're going to make *sure* of it.

SUMMER HEATWAVE
Why not move north?
PAGE 3

PIGS!
They really like mud.
PAGE 15

DAILY BUGLE

MYSTERY
POWER
TEENAGERS
RANSACK BOROUGH

see page 2

TRAFFIC!
You're part of it.
PAGE 11

FORTUNE COOKIES
Not actually from Asia
PAGE 5

And there is it.

Roxxon Secret Laboratories. Today.

What would you have me do?

I told you that I could have members of my team out there hunting, but you--

We could go now.

That's not what I *pay you* to do, Dr. Miller!!

You're scientists... not bounty hunters.

I understand that, but we *have* skills that might get the job done.

No.

Then why are you here?

Mr. Roxxon, you're not seeing the big picture here.

You have-- we have brought you *amazing* results.

Are you not *in awe* of what we discovered here??!!

We took two comatose, half-dead teenagers and created walking, talking portals of energy unlike anything we have ever *seen* on this planet.

Have you seen this, Dr. Miller?

We knew it was coming.

We knew this *exact thing* was going to happen.

We didn't know where or when.

We are *exposed.*

I--I am exposed!!

Because I want you to feel the severity of our situation.

I want you to see how *angry* I am.

Sir--

I didn't get where I am in this world by being *sloppy.*

No sir.

None of us did.

You be quiet, Sterns.

You're lucky you're still alive. On numerous levels.

In fact, I remember you specifically telling me nothing like this would *ever* happen again.

And yet... ever since I let you put this brain trust together, my organization--

This isn't some broken-down Hulk or symbiote!

This is the greatest discovery of what the human machine is capable of.

This is miles ahead of *anything* Reed Richards did.

They make the Fantastic Four look like, you know, the-the Defenders.

Except where are they?

Well done, Lana.

Now try it again with a little finesse.

Uh, what just *happened*?

It would seem you exploded, my dear.

You're a bomb.

Wait, I did that?

See if you can do it on purpose?

I'm a bomb??

Was I *supposed* to be a bomb?

You're an experiment, darling.

Are you a mutant?

I'm not a mutant!! Don't even *go* there!

Where did you get your powers from?

My mom.

Ugh!!

It's a *long* story!

You need help and we want to help you.

We think there's some bad stuff going down and--

"Bad stuff?" Really?

How old are *you*?

How do I look?

I met the first Spider-Man, you know.

No way he would have missed shooting me with a web like *you* did.

Well, I'm just a little-- *AGH!*

What's happening?

Spider-senses.

Yeah me too.

We better--

Yeah.

What is--?

CLANG

Wait, what is that?

27

Then I think it's okay to admit that we're just teenagers and we're in way over our head and we don't know what we--

BOOM

We should--

Yeah, I was just thinking that.

**Brooklyn,
Nine Minutes Ago.**

And why did I give up being Spider-Man?

Oh yeah, stuff like this.

I don't know who this guy is or *how* he found us or *what* he wants or how he has us all *paralyzed*.

(Which feels very freaky weird, by the way.)

Agh!

Aow!

HUUM!

I can't even move my mouth to ask--wait!!

What is he doing?

The *new* Spider-Man.

I bet I could turn this intel into a retirement.

Oh no.

He's going for my mask.

I can't move. I-I can't even blink.

He's got me.

ZZAAAATTT

How is he doing this?

Ah!

What *the hell,* kid?!

You booby-trapped or--

Lucky!

Gargh!

SMMAAASSH

Lucky.

This is going to--

Kid's a natural.

I can't believe I have to drag him back into super-hero-ing kicking and screaming.

Wash happenin'?

CRA

SSSHH

If this Bombshell girl can open up some--no!

She's running away?! You selfish swear-word!

Get up! Come on.

Gotta call S.H.I.E.L.D. and find out what the deal on this guy is.

And where did he get this banned Hydra paralysis tech?

So illegal.

Uh-oh.

Uh, help!

THWIP

CRASSH

Ow!!

And this reminds me of *another* reason I gave up being a super hero.

S.H.I.E.L.D.? Wow.

Pfftt!

Ha!

Aaaaacome on!!

SHOOM SHOOM SHOOM

Guy's big and jacked. And fast.

Unnaturally.

As in he's either a mutant or--

WHACK

SMAACK

SMACCK

SPACK

Nice.

Thanks.

That wasn't so...

Um...

Hard.

Um...

Oh, %©$#!

Yeah.

No!!

Please no, God!!

Please don't let her die anything like this.

This is my fault-- I had no idea he could do that.

One of the growing *list* of reasons why I didn't want to be a super hero in the first place!!

He took my power and slammed you with it.

THWIP

Nice save.

Kid's got real talent.

What a waste.

Come on.

Can you hear me?

Please don't be dead.

THWIP

THWAP

THWAP

THWIP

THWIP

AAGH!!

Nice save, guys! Sorry I panicked and--

Get out of here, Bombshell!!

He's a power absorber!!

We're feeding him power and-- uh-oh.

Uh hi, guys.

Wow, Spider-Man.

You guys again!

Came here for *round two*?! Because I will %○$&@*#--

That *might* have been a misunderstanding.

Ya think?

We didn't know if you *worked* for Roxxon or if you--

Roxxon?

Wait, hold on...

Did--did you just *eat* that guy?

I don't *think* so.

Because it looks like--

Hold on.

There he is.

Who *is* this guy?

Who are *you* guys?

I know we got off on the wrong foot, Lana, but I think you and I/we are in the same boat.

I'm in a boat?

His name is Anthony Masters.

According to his texts-- they call him Taskmaster.

Are we supposed to know him?

Who sent him?

I think I know.

But I'm looking for proof.

And there it is... Roxxon.

This was a contract killing.

Roxxon. Roxxon sent him here to kill *me*?

But he didn't know *we* were going to be here.

This--this is all the proof I needed.

I don't care what S.H.I.E.L.D. and Roxxon are working on together.

I don't care *who* they have donated to politically. I don't care.

I'm not an Ultimate. I'm not a S.H.I.E.L.D. agent. As of now, I'm off the grid.

This is just good guys taking out bad guys.

You guys want in?

What's the plan exactly?

I'm gonna pull Roxxon's world down around his ears while he watches.

The police are here.

Good...

Roxxon Industries.

Mr. Roxxon, you need to come with us right now!

What is it? What has happened?

It's Spider-Man, sir.

Spider-Man? He's *here*?!

They intercepted Taskmaster.

Intercepted? Who intercepted?

Our man in the field says it didn't go.

He observed from a distance as requested.

He says they are headed here *right now*. Directly.

(What I paid Taskmaster.)

Sir, please.

I thought Spider-Man was no longer an ongoing concern! I thought he retired!

Sir, I'm telling you what I--

They? You said *they*? Who is *they*?

There's a handful of, um, characters with him.

We're still getting Intel but...

How many?

Sir, I need to get you off the premises but you have to--

Oh no.

Do not fire until I say.

Sir?

Call my science team up here *now*.

Your *science* team? Sir, we are your security and we can--

The brain trust. Get them up here now.

I can handle this!

I haven't been Spider-Man in about a year, so I'm a little rusty with the snappy things you're supposed to say at just such a moment.

Don't take it personally.

WHACK

Are these the evil scientists?

They call themselves the brain trust.

Are these the ones that turned you into... this?

Yes.

Then I don't feel bad about kicking a girl in the face.

I'm a girl. I'm ruling it okay.

No one listens to me...

I forgot to tell you that the old guy can turn into...

Well, you can see it...

That--
that didn't
go bad at
all.

EVERYONE
FREEZE!

KREEEEEE

Billionaire.
Genius.
Superhero.

Addict.

The story of Tony Stark.

Peter Biskind

TONY STARK
MAN
OF
IRON

Dude.

Sshh!

Dude,
are--are
you--

Ganke,
whisper.

Are you--
are you *back*?
Are you, you know,
him again?

Just
listen...

I'm sorry
I was being like
that and I'm sorry
I was making
you mad.

You were
right.

Thank you
for hanging in
there with me.

Just, you
know, thank
you.

For
everything.

Aw...
Dude.

Just tell
me you're back
for real.

Tell me
this is for
real.

I'm telling
you...you're
right, Ganke.

You
were totally
right.

Dad?

"Maybe ask your father about 'the old days.'

"Maybe ask your father about who he was before you were born."

"So obviously I was a little surprised that you went on a little field trip to Roxxon Industries without even a 'by your leave.'

"What do you have to say for yourself?"

Director Chang, for the record I had hard intelligence that the Roxxon Corporation had kidnapped underage American citizens and experimented on them using untested genetic technology.

I acted accordingly.

In pursuit I was assaulted by a mercenary code-named Taskmaster hired by Roxxon.

After subduing the mercenary, I thought it was in the best interest of all concerned that we act quickly.

I am willing to testify to all of this under oath so that the Roxxon Corporation is put down for good once and for all.

You did all that, did you?

Do you know that we do business with the Roxxon Corporation? That we have standing military contracts?

That is above my pay grade, ma'am.

I'm sure that if you knew Roxxon was kidnapping children and experimenting on them you would cease all business.

And who were these children you had deputized for your operation?

So very glad you asked.

I think we have something here...

I think we have the beginnings of something very special.

The End
Next: Cataclysm!